GREY
AREA

Preface

I started writing when I was 13, my mental health deteriorating over the years. I would seek help from school counsellors, but besides providing me a safe space to talk, nothing was done to improve my health.

After a series of mentally traumatic incidents between the years 2015 and 2016, my mental health rapidly declined. I had attempted suicide twice in 2018, and only then did I decide to put a stop in my pursuit of a bachelor's degree to seek help in therapy.

I am a very happy person. I love to joke and have fun with my friends. However, mental illness does not simply glide over anyone in a fit of laughter.

Grey Area is a collection of poetry and prose documenting my struggle with mental illness from the time I was 13 to the present time. I do advise readers to take a break after reading a couple of works.

In memory of my mum:
Don't rest in peace,
Rock it like you did on Earth!

Fein

I put on a warm smile
But I am frowning
The pain is killing
But I must not show it

I put up a strong front
But to show weakness, I can't
It hurts, yes it does
But no, I must conquer

I take a deep breath
As I confront the inevitable
No, I must not stumble
No, the fortress must not crumble

Like daggers stabbing into my heart
No, I must not die
I must subdue it
I must numb it

Escape

Let me out
Let me breathe
Not another burden to heave
Let me leave

Set me free
Rescue me
Do I have to flee?
Can you not hear my plea?

Please, I beg you
What do you want me to do?
My heart grows heavier
As my vision gets blurrier

I cannot remain this way
Not forever, can I stay
I will not listen to what you say
I, will run away

Hostility

What are these sounds?
Like the melody of the unworthy
It screams inside of me
It pains me to see this

How I wish it could be mine
Then, the worthy shall outshine
Then, after all this while
I can finally smile

Let me look into your soul
But then, why are you so cold?
You have nothing to lose
It's up to you, so chose

I glare into your hostility
As you take advantage of my vulnerability
I will keep this up
Until you give up

Blind

It's heaviness
Weighing down on me
It blinds me
I can't see

Happiness I sense
Yet happiness I do not feel
How long would it take
For my wounds to heal?

Always, always
My eyes are brimming with tears
Ready to burst
All these days

Nothing, no one
Can help me out of this
This searing pain inside of me
That blinds me, I can't see.

Space

Like the vastness of the ocean
As if it never ended
If there was no betrayal
Beyond which can never be comprehended

Like the never ending expanse of the sky
If it ever ended, no one would cry
As if it ever ended, everyone would die
Saying sorry, it's just one big lie

Like the open of a field
Unprotected, no shield
Strength, one cannot yield
Just, keep your lips sealed

In the infinity of the universe
Like the cold darkness of the worst
Stop making me swear and curse
In thy evil, you shall immerse

Struggle

I sleep, I sleep
But I weep, I weep
Of everything I could ever want
Of everything I could never need

I envision the darkness cloaking the light
The light in which tells of my plight
Like the last light casting the shadows
Like light that never enters my windows

I am bounded by ropes of anger
I am enraged by countless attacks
But everyone has a common gain
But that gain is lost in vain

It is the heart that most blinds us
Yet it is the heart that causes us to see
Of anyone who could set us free
It is neither them nor they, it is only

Envelope

The accumulating pressure surrounds me
It strangles me, I can't breathe
It forces tears from me, I can't see
Too heavy a burden to heave

Like a knife
Ripping through me
This searing pain
I'm going insane

I falter, it sensed it so
An opportunity
It seized me
I fall

Trapped, shackled.
This pain, the same.
The pain my tears once trickled
Returned.

Desperation

I tremble in fear
As the inevitable draws near
My eyes, they tear
My ears, strain to hear

My heart races
My blood surges
I can't face it
I have fallen into a pit

I cannot take it anymore
I hate it to the core
It is such an eyesore
Not anymore, can I implore

I fall to my knees
As no one hears my pleas
I tremble and shake
What does all this make?

Hurry Up Please, It's Time.

Crinkle

My head is already heavy;
Or am I lightheaded?

Crinkle

It hurts to breathe;
Already?

Crinkle

I bow my head as I blank out my thoughts.
HURRY UP PLEASE ITS TIME.

Sliding the bubble of death over my face
I tune out the senseless chatter of regret.
HURRY UP PLEASE ITS TIME.

I do not take note of how long it has been
As I stare into the face of me.
HURRY UP PLEASE ITS TIME.

Rescue

When will it all end?
I am trying so hard to dream
All I hear is the impending doom
Oh, please rescue me from this gloom

My eyes glare into the distance
As I wince at the blinding eternity
Of never ending inferiority
I reach out and grasp onto sorrow

It is this fate that has arrested me
I struggle as I weep in pain
I cannot feel anything
And neither can I see

I am numbed as is my mind
Pain I do not feel
Hurt I always have
Of everything I could never find

Dreamed Reality

The person I looked to for direction
With instructions I did not follow with caution
I did not stop to think
Until reality began to sink

I am numbed
I am shackled
This was the pain
That my tears trickled

Again a return to reality,
It is the heart that most blinds us.
And out of my pleasant reverie,
Yet it is the heart that causes us to see.

All my hopes are shattered
Where my dreams have once been
Where my love has once been seen
When it was there, and all could see.

Sorrow

In the glow of the midnight moon
Shadows are cast across the valley of gloom
Where light is absent
No one can sense the darkness' presence

A violent red
Drawn with thy blood
If anyone knew, it wouldn't be said
If anyone knew, they would've been dead

A chamber where light didn't reach
Where sorrow clings on like a leach
Blood thirsty creatures
Where light never reaches

Time, one cannot borrow
A path, one cannot follow
It is my fault, I know
But, must I be laden with pain and sorrow?

Gloom

I'm lost, I'm confused
I'm hoping for this situation to defuse
I'm exhausted, I'm tired
And I have nothing left to be desired

I'm angry, I'm frustrated
My patience, abated
I'm scared, I'm fearful
And I need no one else but you

I'm nervous, I'm anxious
Your voice, so precious
I'm sad, I'm depressed
And this, I detest

I'm hurt, in pain
I'm waiting in vain
I'm miserable, in sorrow
Time, I'd like to borrow

Ash

Grey are the grains that sift through this
hourglass.
Cremated in the timeline of bitterness,
Lies the power I once held.

For how long is this memory of once unbroken
trust
Going to sit there?
The ashened face of this sobering reality;
Too crude to confront.

Burning on the bridge of trust
My integrity shattered.
Like the grey ash of fate that is now settling,
So are my tears that once trickled;
As I watch the lifeless ash sift through this
hourglass of bitterness.

There Was Nothing

What is "Nothing"?
Is it the absence of "Something"?
Is it emptiness?
Or is it the silence that holds me?

Is there really "Nothing"?
Would space be considered "Something"?
Is it tangible?
Or is it the air that I cannot breathe?

I have nothing.
Yet, "having" implies I do have "something".
Is it something I said?
Or was it something I did not say?

Freedom cannot be seen.
Yet we all want it.
Do I have it?
Or do I have an illusion of it?
Is it something?
Is it nothing?
What is "Nothing"?

My Love,
My Anger

How do you even begin to describe it?
It makes you sick in the stomach.
Your steps, increasingly heavy.
Thoughts of violence and revenge flood your
mind.

Why are you angry?
Free yourself from its grasp.
You will feel better.
I'm scared.

I'm afraid of the things I am capable of achieving.
I'm afraid of the dreams that will come true.
Because I'm scared.

This anger defines me, and without it,
People will forget who I really am.

In Power

Look around you,
What do you see?
Do we all look the same?
Or is it just me?

For you to choose this path,
Screams incompetent.
For you to abuse this power,
Screams dominant.

You only think you have nothing to lose,
But only because I have nothing to choose.
You let yourself forget,
That people are not mere puppets.

Would you ever learn to handle the truth,
Or are they just wounds for you to soothe?
Do not abuse this power any longer,
For those like me will only grow stronger.

Empathy

I want everyone to know how I feel;
For me to see the fear in their eyes.
The beads of sweat that drip down their faces;
Like the tears of blood that I once cried.
I did not want to go through it alone,
But I did. Unwilling, and bounded.
It was not till the first seed was sown;
I was trapped, and all alone.

Now, like rock beneath the Earth;
My body has become like stone.
Every part aching in anger.
I try to breathe.
But I can't, no longer;
And I want you to be tortured.

Sit down, and take a look;
Not around you, but into
My eyes as I rip
Your spine from your beliefs.
As you crumble and twist,
With my eyes locked into yours,
You will become like stone;
Like me;

But not alone.

It's All In My Head

I wish it were that simple.
Focus on the positive things.
Just don't think about it.
People have it worse than I do.

I wish it were that simple.
The agonising pain I go through.
Every single muscle in my body;
Aching with death.

I wish it were that simple.
The screaming in my head.
The voices that don't exist.
The visions you don't see.

I wish it were that simple.
Controlled by a tiny pill.
Struggling to live.
Not a choice.

I were it was that simple.
To control the screaming in my head,
To control the voices you don't hear.
For you to understand how I feel.

Comfort In Pain

I have been left in this chamber for so long;
It is not a home to me,
But a second skin.
What would I bleed if I shed this skin?

The scars that no one sees.
Wounds I worked hard to heal.
Yet,
I have been left in this chamber for so long;
I cannot bare to see what lies outside.

When I am finally rescued from this cage;
No one can force me to come out.
Would I want to be met with the unfamiliar?
Or would I be dragged back into the cage,
Where the pain continues?

It feels only right to hurt.
I have been left in this chamber for so long;
I have grown used to the shackles.
This second skin that I wear,
Bound to me and controls me.

The Power
I Hold

I know the power I potentially hold,
But I do not know how I would be able to control it.
Every day that I am weak,
Makes me want that power to consume me.
To control me.
The only thing I know that can control that power
Is power from external forces.
Yet people don't believe the power that I hold.
The power that I've been suppressing for years.
The power that I thought people shouldn't see.
Yet,
Every day that I am weak,
Those who surround me constantly make me
tempted.
Tempted to let that power return.
Tempted to show them what anger really means.
The tears of weakness are nothing.
Nothing as compared to the destruction of anger.
The anger that the power I hold is overwhelming.
Because every day I suppress it,
It grows.

Perhaps one day,
It will grow to be insuppressible.
And when that day comes,
I will still be weak,
But weak in the sense that
I will not be able to suppress my power any longer.
That power will make me weaker, yet powerful.

Look into my eyes,
See me begging you internally.
I am screaming in silence.
I am on my knees.
My tears of weakness can no longer controlled.
I am getting weaker.
And one day I will no longer be strong enough to
remain weak.
And when that day comes,
The power that I hold will be overwhelming.
I know the power I potentially hold,
But I do not know how I would be able to control it.

The Mask Of Ignorance

It's an interesting, yet saddening feeling.
How I can be surrounded by people,
But still, I'm lonely.
Yet, these people will never harm me.
Maybe it's because they don't know my past.
Maybe it's because they won't be part of my
future.
Even though they're there at present,
I feel myself being trapped in a constant rewind.
My past.
Those who knew me would know the danger I
pose.
The mask of ignorance I am wearing,
My last line of defence against my own power.

The mask of ignorance is a powerful one.
With it, I don't listen to the things I hear.
I don't notice the things I see.
But like every line of defence there is,
It won't last.
There is no way to make it stronger,
Because with every bullet of assumption,
Every arrow of dishonesty,
It gets weaker.
I start to listen to the things I hear.
I begin to notice the things I see.
The pain I've numbed
Cannot be ignored forever.

The violence in my mind is unimaginable.
Because I would have just let it run;
In the past.
But I've seen the destruction it can cause,
I've once held the power I hold.
Yet behind the mask of ignorance I wear,
No one in my present believes me,
When I try to warn them about that power.
Are they encouraging me to let it return?
Do they not understand the damage it has done
And what it could possibly do?
Do they have to see it for themselves before
acknowledging it?
Do I have to remove the mask of ignorance?
It's an interesting, yet saddening feeling.
How I can be surrounded by people,
But still, I'm lonely.
Yet, these people will never harm me.
Maybe it's because they don't know my past.
Maybe it's because they won't be part of my
future.
Even though they're there at present,
I feel myself being trapped in a constant rewind.
My past.

www.ingramcontent.com/pod-product-compliance
Lightning Source LLC
Chambersburg PA
CBHW022041090426
42741CB00007B/1158